OH! MY
KOREAN
TUTORS

Yoonjun Kim | Hyunju Nam | Gail Yoon | Seonkyong Lee

OH! MY KOREAN TUTORS

Seoul Selection

INTRODUCTION

● Oh! My Korean Tutors

Oh! My Korean Tutors is a book for beginners in Korean—people who are dipping their toes into this fascinating language. It was sparked by the desire to make Korean easier and more fun for those just getting started. From the moment you open the cover, this book is designed to act as a cheerful tutor who will aid you in your study of Korean. So join us on a gentle journey into the Korean language. Don't worry! We'll take things one step at a time.

● The perfect Korean language textbook for beginners

Don't start off learning Hangeul (the Korean script) by taking on something too challenging at the very beginning. A few simple formulas will make it easy to understand enough Korean to get you started.

• This book is carefully organized around four stages of learning that will help you quickly grasp Korean consonants, vowels and essential vocabulary for daily life. We also include figures that will unlock the mysteries of the Hangeul writing system. Each unit ends with a game that will review what you've learned.
• This book will not only guide you through the Korean language but also through intriguing facets of Korean life and culture. These fascinating snapshots of Korean culture will give you a refreshing break from your study of Hangeul.

• Step by step, this book will teach you the grammatical expressions and vocabulary needed to introduce yourself to Koreans. By the end of the book, you'll be ready to make a simple self-introduction in the Korean language.

Beginning your Korean studies with this book will teach you all the basic skills needed to stride confidently ahead in your study of the language.
We also believe this book will be very handy for teachers of introductory Korean courses looking for novel approaches to teaching the language.

TABLE OF CONTENTS

Introducing Yourself

BOOK LAYOUT

Part	Chapter	Topic	Contents
Learning Hangeul	1. Vowels and Consonants	1) Vowels and Consonants 1	ㅏ, ㅓ, ㅗ, ㅜ, ㅡ, ㅣ ㄱ, ㄴ, ㅁ, ㅅ, ㅇ
		2) Vowels and Consonants 2	ㅑ, ㅕ, ㅛ, ㅠ ㄷ, ㄹ, ㅂ, ㅈ
		3) Vowels and Consonants 3	ㅐ, ㅔ, ㅒ, ㅖ, ㅢ ㅊ, ㅋ, ㅌ, ㅍ, ㅎ
		4) Vowels and Consonants 4	ㅘ, ㅙ, ㅚ ㄲ, ㄸ, ㅃ, ㅆ, ㅉ
		5) Vowels and Consonants 5	ㅝ, ㅞ, ㅟ ㄱ, ㄴ, ㄷ, ㄹ, ㅁ, ㅂ, ㅅ, ㅇ, ㅈ, ㅊ, ㅋ, ㅌ, ㅍ, ㅎ, ㄲ, ㄸ, ㅃ, ㅆ, ㅉ
	2. Syllables	6) Syllables	(1) □ V (2) C V (3) V C V C C (4) C V C C V C C
	3. Final consonants	7) Final consonants 1	ㄱ, ㅋ, ㄲ/ ㄴ, ㄹ, ㅁ/ ㅂ, ㅍ
		8) Final consonants 2	ㄷ, ㅅ, ㅆ, ㅈ, ㅊ, ㅌ, ㅎ / ㅇ
		9) Final consonants 3	ㄳ, ㄵ, ㄶ, ㄼ, ㄽ, ㄾ, ㅀ, ㅄ/ ㄺ, ㄻ, ㄿ

USING THIS BOOK

Oh! My Korean Tutors is divided into three main sections: 1) The Story of Hangeul, 2) Learning Hangeul, and 3) Introducing Yourself.

The Story of Hangeul introduces readers to Hangeul, the Korean writing system.

Learning Hangeul is made up of several units, each with their own grammar and writing sections, as well as practice exercises that include listening and repeating, dictation, and games.

Introducing Yourself consists of the simple grammar constructions and vocabulary needed for making a self-introduction, along with practice exercises. At certain points in the book, we take a break from our studies to examine various aspects of Korean culture.

Learning Hangeul

• Today's Study Plan

The learning material for each unit is detailed here.

• Listening

This part can give you an idea about what you'll be studying.

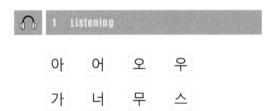

• Today's Lesson

The target grammar is expressed through formulas that help you easily visualize the information.

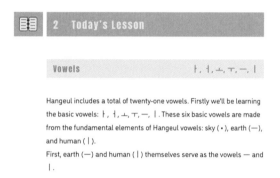

This QR code links to a lecture about the study material.

USING THIS BOOK

• Writing Practice

Review what you've learned through writing exercises.

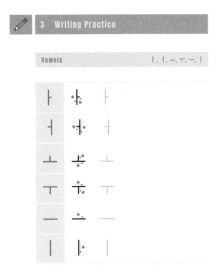

• Vocabulary

You can practice listening to, speaking, and writing various vocabulary words via the QR codes.

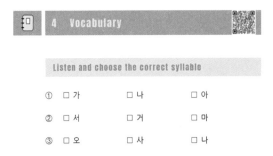

• Let's play a game

Solve the problems and check the answers. This is an enjoyable way to review the vocabulary you've learned.

Let's play a game

In the box below, find all the words made up of the consonants and vowels we learned today. (There are five altogether, not including the two examples shown in blue below.)

거	두	나	무	쿠	시
미	보	후	이	지	소
베	퍼	히	누	제	이
아	이	다	나	바	호
고	구	마	스	디	키
데	파	비	어	머	니

Introducing Yourself

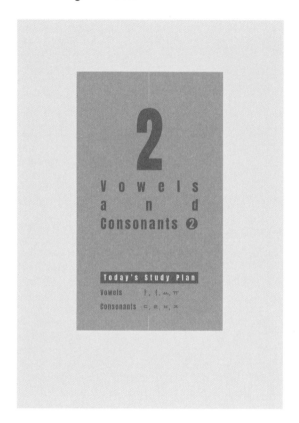

• Today's Study Plan

The learning material for each area is detailed here.

• Today's Lesson

Through these simple dialogues, you can learn the grammar needed to introduce yourself one step at a time.

We draw your attention to potential pitfalls to make sure you use grammar correctly.

1 Today's Lesson

This is how to tell someone your name in Korean.

이름이 뭐예요?
What is your name?

저는 스테판이에요.
I am Stephen.

Grammar 1   이름이 뭐예요?

이름이 뭐예요?
What is your name?

저는 스테판이에요.
I am Stephen.

이름이 뭐예요?
What is your name?

제 이름은 김누리예요.
My name is Nuri Kim.

만나서 반가워요.
Nice to meet you.

만나서 반가워요.
Nice to meet you.

USING THIS BOOK

• Vocabulary

A list of words is provided to help you master the vocabulary needed for each unit.

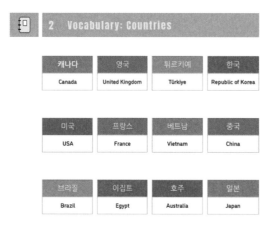

• Introducing Yourself

Repeated practice can give you a natural command of the material you've learned.

● What is Hangeul?

Hangeul is the name of the official writing system designed to represent the Korean language. Just as English has the alphabet, Korean has Hangeul.

In 1443, King Sejong of the Joseon Dynasty created and promulgated a writing system called Hunminjeongeum, meaning the "proper sounds for instructing the people." Since the early 20th century, Hunminjeongeum has been referred to as Hangeul. Based on the interpretation of its Chinese characters, "Hangeul" can be defined in several ways: a great writing system, the only writing system, and Koreans' writing system.

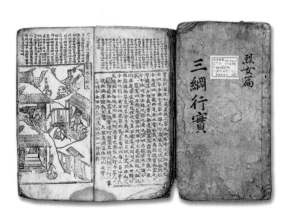 

Samgang haengsildo (삼강행실도)ː A moral guide created with illustrations and Hunminjeongeum (Korean script) to teach the common people.
Image source: Korea Heritage Service (국가유산포털)

King Sejong produced many books for the people, but those written in Chinese characters were of no use to people who couldn't read them. This highlighted the need for a simple script of the Korean language that ordinary people could easily learn.

● The intriguing characters of Hunminjeongeum

Hangeul is the only writing system in the world for which we know the author, the date of publication, and even the principles by which the characters were made.

The Hunminjeongeum commentaries (one volume of 33 woodblocks that explain in detail the principles of Hangeul and the purpose for its creation) were inscribed on the UNESCO Memory of the World in 1997. The South Korean government celebrates the creation of Hangeul on October 9, the date of its promulgation, which was designated Hangeul Day.

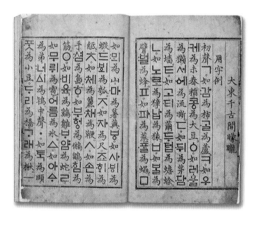 

Hunminjeongeum Haeryebon (The Proper Sounds for the Instruction of the People): A book explaining the principles and usage of Hangeul, created by King Sejong. Scholars from Jiphyeonjeon (the Hall of Worthies) provided commentary in Classical Chinese.
Image source: Korea Heritage Service (국가유산포털)

● Principles behind the creation of Hunminjeongeum

"All human speech also possesses the principles of yin and yang,
  but people simply never bothered to examine that."

  - King Sejong

Korean consonants were constructed according to the philosophical idea of the five elements*, while Korean vowels were constructed from three shapes: a dot (•) representing the sky, a horizontal line (—) representing the flat earth, and a vertical line (|) representing a human standing upright.

---

* The five elements, or *ohaeng* in Korean, refer to the ancient Asian philosophical belief that everything in the universe consisted of five basic elements: wood, fire, earth, metal, and water.

● Initial position (Consonant)

The design of Korean consonants was inspired by the shape of the mouth when speaking and the place of articulation in the mouth. Each basic consonant shape is modified with additional strokes to indicate various phonetic changes.

For example, the consonant ㄱ (g/k) becomes ㅋ (kʰ) with the addition of a stroke or ㄲ (k') through duplication of the initial shape.

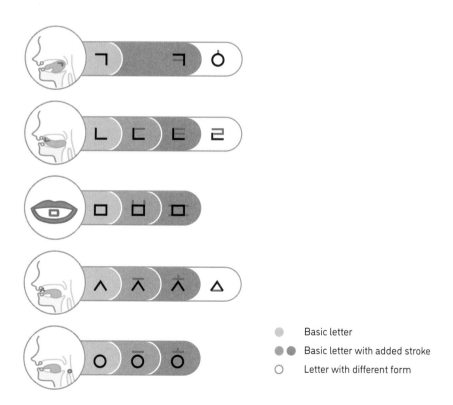

⬤   Basic letter

⬤⬤   Basic letter with added stroke

◯   Letter with different form

● Middle position (Vowel)

As mentioned above, Korean vowels
are made from a combination of a dot
(•) representing the sky, a horizontal
line (一) representing the ground,
and a vertical line (|) representing
a human standing upright. This form
is sometimes called *cheonjiin* (천지
인), based on the Chinese characters
"天地人," meaning "sky, earth, and
human."

The three elements of sky (•), earth (一), and human (|) can be
combined to create a variety of vowels. Note that vowels with one dot
(•) are called single vowels while vowels with two dots (•) are called
diphthongs.

| | + • = | • → ㅏ |

| • + 一 = ·一 → ㅗ |

● Final consonant

A consonant is used in the final position, just as in the initial position.

● Syllables

A Korean syllable refers to the character formed by combining an initial consonant, middle vowel, and an optional final consonant. The middle vowel is placed either below or to the right of the initial consonant. If the character contains a final consonant, it is placed below the initial and middle letters. In its final written form, a character of Hangeul should always form a regular square, just as Chinese characters do.

● Hangeul writing order

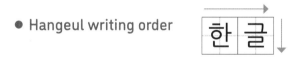

Completed syllables are written from left to right, as are the first consonant, middle vowel, and optional final consonant.

Tutor's tip ! In this book, the text boxes for writing Hangeul ☐ include dotted lines in the form of a cross ⊞ to help you write your characters correctly.

Learning

Hangeul

1

Vowels and Consonants ❶

Today's Study Plan

Vowels ㅏ, ㅓ, ㅗ, ㅜ, ㅡ, ㅣ

Consonants ㄱ, ㄴ, ㅁ, ㅅ, ㅇ

1 Listening

아 어 오 우

가 너 무 스

 2 Today's Lesson

Vowels　　　　　　　　ㅏ, ㅓ, ㅗ, ㅜ, ㅡ, ㅣ

Hangeul includes a total of twenty-one vowels. Firstly we'll be learning the basic vowels: ㅏ, ㅓ, ㅗ, ㅜ, ㅡ, ㅣ. These six basic vowels are made from the fundamental elements of Hangeul vowels: sky (•), earth (ㅡ), and human (ㅣ).

First, earth (ㅡ) and human (ㅣ) themselves serve as the vowels ㅡ and ㅣ.

 →

 →

28

Those two elements are combined with sky (•) to make the following vowels.

| │ | + | • | = | │• | → | ├ |

| • | + | │ | = | •│ | → | ┤ |

| • | + | — | = | •over— | → | ⊥ |

| — | + | • | = | —over• | → | ┬ |

So how are these vowels pronounced and written?

Vowels	IPA	Stroke order	Mouth shape
ㅏ	[a]		
ㅓ	[ə]		
ㅗ	[o]		
ㅜ	[u]		
ㅡ	[ɯ]		
ㅣ	[i]		

Tutor's tip! While vowels can make a sound even without a consonant, vowels must be written with consonants to form syllables in the Hangeul writing system. When a syllable only has a vowel sound, the vowel is written along with the consonant ㅇ (ŋ) that acts as a silent placeholder.

Examples: 아, 어, 오, 우, 으, 이

Hangeul has a total of nineteen consonants, five of which are regarded as basic consonants. Those five are inspired by the shape and placement of the articulators. The five basic consonants that we'll be learning in this unit are ㄱ, ㄴ, ㅁ, ㅅ, ㅇ.

Let's see how these consonants are pronounced and written.

Consonants	Name	IPA	Stroke order
ㄱ	기역 [giyeok]	[k/g]	
ㄴ	니은 [nieun]	[n]	
ㅁ	미음 [mieum]	[m]	
ㅅ	시옷 [siot]	[s]	
ㅇ	이응 [ieung]	[ŋ]	

Vowel + Consonant

Hangeul is a writing system in which vowels and consonants are written together. Vowels either appear to the right or the bottom of the initial consonant (including the silent ㅇ), depending on their shape.

(1) The vowels ㅏ, ㅓ, and ㅣ are placed to the right of the initial consonant.

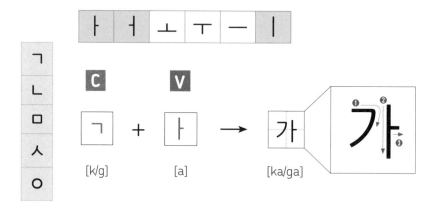

(2) The vowels ㅗ, ㅜ, and ㅡ are placed to the bottom of the initial consonant.

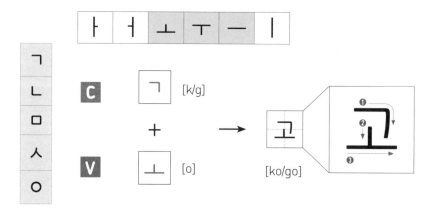

(3) Take a look at the syllables formed by combining six basic vowels (ㅏ, ㅓ, ㅗ, ㅜ, ㅡ, ㅣ) with the silent ㅇ.

(4) Here are the syllables that are formed when we combine the six basic vowels (ㅏ, ㅓ, ㅗ, ㅜ, ㅡ, ㅣ) with the five basic consonants (ㄱ, ㄴ, ㅁ, ㅅ, ㅇ).

Vowels   ㅏ, ㅓ, ㅗ, ㅜ, ㅡ, ㅣ

ㅏ	ㅏ	ㅏ			
ㅓ	ㅓ	ㅓ			
ㅗ	ㅗ	ㅗ			
ㅜ	ㅜ	ㅜ			
ㅡ	ㅡ	ㅡ			
ㅣ	ㅣ	ㅣ			

ㄱ	ㄱ	ㄱ			
ㄴ	ㄴ	ㄴ			
ㅁ	ㅁ	ㅁ			
ㅅ	ㅅ	ㅅ			
ㅇ	ㅇ	ㅇ			

	ㅏ	ㅓ	ㅗ	ㅜ	ㅡ	ㅣ
ㄱ	가					
ㄴ		너				
ㅁ			모			
ㅅ				수		
ㅇ					으	

36

4　Vocabulary

Listen and choose the correct syllable

① ☐ 가　　☐ 나　　☐ 아

② ☐ 서　　☐ 거　　☐ 마

③ ☐ 오　　☐ 사　　☐ 나

Listen and repeat the following words

① 나 I　　② 너 You　　③ 거미 Spider

④ 가구 Furniture　　⑤ 이 Two / Teeth　　⑥ 오 Five

Listen and choose the correct answer

① ☐ 너무 Too, so　　☐ 나무 Tree

② ☐ 아니 No　　☐ 아이 Child, Kid

③ ☐ 거기 There　　☐ 고기 Meat

Listen and write the following words

① 고구마 Sweet potato

② 누나 Older sister

③ 이마 Forehead

④ 시소 Seesaw

⑤ 어머니 Mother

Let's play a game

In the box below, find all the words made up of the consonants and vowels we learned today. (There are five altogether, not including the two examples shown in blue below.)

거	두	나	무	쿠	시
미	보	후	이	지	소
베	퍼	히	누	제	이
아	이	다	나	바	호
고	구	마	스	디	키
데	파	비	어	머	니

2

Vowels
and
Consonants ②

Vowels   ㅑ, ㅕ, ㅛ, ㅠ

Consonants ㄷ, ㄹ, ㅂ, ㅈ

야	여	요	유
댜	벼	죠	류

 2 **Today's Lesson**

Vowels ㅑ, ㅕ, ㅛ, ㅠ

In the previous section, we learned the vowels ㅏ, ㅓ, ㅗ, ㅜ, ㅡ, ㅣ. The vowels ㅏ, ㅓ, ㅗ, ㅜ can be combined with the element (•) to make ㅑ, ㅕ, ㅛ, ㅠ.

ㅏ ㅓ ㅗ ㅜ	+	•	=	 	→	ㅑ ㅕ ㅛ ㅠ

Here's how these vowels are pronounced and written.

Vowels	IPA	Stroke order
ㅑ	[ya]	
ㅕ	[yə]	
ㅛ	[yo]	
ㅠ	[yu]	

The basic consonants of Hangeul can be used to make even more consonants. There are two ways of doing that:

(1) adding strokes to the basic consonant

(2) adding consonant to another consonant

Here, we will learn how strokes are added to four of the five basic consonants (ㄴ, ㅁ, ㅅ, ㅇ) to make the consonants ㄷ, ㅂ, ㅈ, ㆆ.

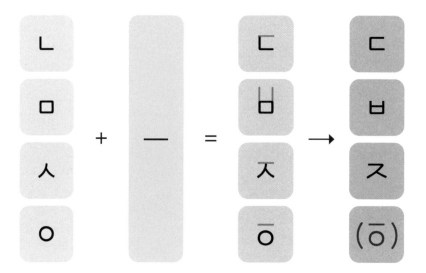

Tutor's tip! The consonant ㆆ, which is made by adding a stroke to ㅇ, is not currently in use. The reason we've included it in this table is to help you learn a consonant in the next stage.

Let's see how these consonants are pronounced and written.

Consonants	Name	IPA	Stroke order
ㄷ	디귿 [digeut]	[t/d]	
ㅂ	비읍 [bieup]	[p/b]	
ㅈ	지읒 [jieut]	[ts/dz]	

Consonants	Name	IPA	Stroke order
ㄹ	리을 [ri-eul]	[l/r]	

(1) The vowels ㅑ and ㅕ are placed to the right of the initial consonant (including the silent ㅇ).

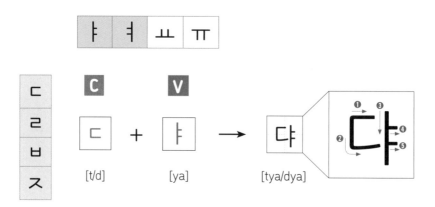

(2) The vowels ㅛ and ㅠ are placed at the bottom of the initial consonant.

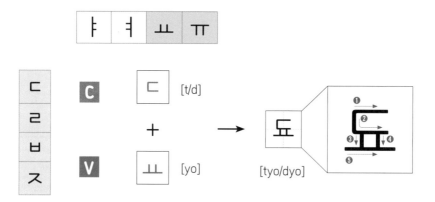

(3) Take a look at the syllables formed when we combine vowels (ㅑ, ㅕ, ㅛ, ㅠ) with the silent ㅇ.

	ㅑ	ㅕ	ㅛ	ㅠ
ㅇ	야	여	요	유

(4) Let's learn which syllables are formed when we combine the vowels (ㅑ, ㅕ, ㅛ, ㅠ) and consonants (ㄷ, ㄹ, ㅂ, ㅈ).

	ㅑ	ㅕ	ㅛ	ㅠ
ㄷ	댜	뎌	됴	듀
ㄹ	랴	려	료	류
ㅂ	뱌	벼	뵤	뷰
ㅈ	쟈	져	죠	쥬

3   Writing Practice

ㅑ	ㅑ	ㅑ		
ㅕ	ㅕ	ㅕ		
ㅛ	ㅛ	ㅛ		
ㅠ	ㅠ	ㅠ		

ㄷ	ㄷ	ㄷ			
ㄹ	ㄹ	ㄹ			
ㅂ	ㅂ	ㅂ			
ㅈ	ㅈ	ㅈ			

Combine the consonants and vowels

	ㅑ	ㅕ	ㅛ	ㅠ
ㄷ	댜			
ㄹ		려		
ㅂ			뵤	
ㅈ				쥬

Listen and choose the correct syllable

① ☐ 댜　☐ 갸　☐ 쟈

② ☐ 려　☐ 료　☐ 류

③ ☐ 쥬　☐ 류　☐ 뷰

Listen and repeat the following words

① 교수 Professor　② 무료 Free of charge　③ 바지 Trousers

④ 기자 Reporter　⑤ 요리 Cooking　⑥ 유리 Glass

Listen and choose the correct answer

① ☐ 우유 Milk　☐ 이유 Reason

② ☐ 여자 Woman　☐ 여우 Fox

③ ☐ 드라마 Drama　☐ 다리미 Iron

Listen and write the following words

① 우유 Milk

② 야구 Baseball

③ 서류 Document

④ 아니요 No

⑤ 주유소 Gas station

Let's play a game

Complete the words with the missing letters.

ㅇ 자	＿라마	이ㅇ
Woman	Drama	Reason
ㅇ 니ㅇ	서ㅠ	무ㄹ
No	Document	Free of charge
ㅇ 우	기 ㅏ	ㅏ지
Fox	Reporter	Trousers

3

Vowels and Consonants ③

Today's Study Plan	
Vowels	ㅐ, ㅔ, ㅒ, ㅖ, ㅢ
Consonants	ㅊ, ㅋ, ㅌ, ㅍ, ㅎ

애	에	얘	예
캐	테	해	폐
의	틔	희	

2 Today's Lesson

Vowels   ㅐ, ㅔ, ㅒ, ㅖ, ㅢ

We've already learned that the element (•) can be added to the vowels ㅏ, ㅓ to make ㅑ, ㅕ and to the vowels ㅗ, ㅜ to make ㅛ, ㅠ. Next, we will learn how the element ㅣ (which is itself a vowel) can be added to the vowels ㅏ, ㅑ, ㅓ, ㅕ, ㅡ to make ㅐ, ㅒ, ㅔ, ㅖ, ㅢ.

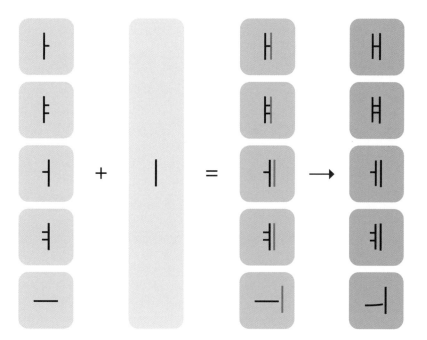

Here's how these vowels are pronounced and written.

Vowels	IPA	Stroke order
ㅐ	[ɛ]	❶ ㅐ ❸ ❷
ㅔ	[e]	❶ ㅔ ❸ ❷
ㅒ	[yɛ]	❶ ㅒ ❹ ❷ ❸
ㅖ	[ye]	❶ ㅖ ❸ ❹ ❷
ㅢ	[ɰi/i]	❶ ㅢ ❷

Tutor's tip!

(1) While vowels can make a sound on their own without a consonant, a syllable that only has a vowel sound must include the silent placeholder ㅇ.

(2) The pronunciation of the vowels ㅐ, ㅔ is nearly the same; even Koreans don't distinguish between them.

(3) The vowel ㅢ can be pronounced as [ɰi], [i], or [e], depending on its position.

We'll now be adding strokes to some of the consonants we've learned. The additional strokes turn ㄱ into ㅋ, ㄷ into ㅌ, ㅂ into ㅍ, ㅈ into ㅊ, and ㆆ into ㅎ. (As mentioned previously, ㆆ is not in current use.)

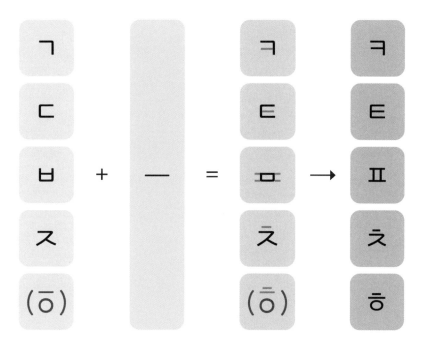

Four of these five consonants (ㅋ, ㅌ, ㅍ, and ㅊ) have a breathier sound than the earlier form. The technical term for them is aspirated consonants.

Let's see how these consonants are pronounced and written.

Consonants	Name	IPA	Stroke order
ㅊ	치읓 [chieut]	[tsʰ]	
ㅋ	키읔 [kieuk]	[kʰ]	
ㅌ	티읕 [tieut]	[tʰ]	
ㅍ	피읖 [pieup]	[pʰ]	
ㅎ	히읗 [hieut]	[h]	

Vowel + Consonant

(1) Take a look at the syllables formed when we combine vowels (ㅐ, ㅔ, ㅒ, ㅖ, ㅢ) with the silent placeholder ㅇ.

(2) Let's learn which syllables are formed when we combine the vowels (ㅐ, ㅔ, ㅒ, ㅖ, ㅢ) and consonants (ㅊ, ㅋ, ㅌ, ㅍ, ㅎ).

Tutor's tip! The gray letters in the above table are not used much in contemporary Korean.

Vowels			ㅐ , ㅔ , ㅒ , ㅖ , ㅢ

ㅐ	ㅐ	ㅐ	
ㅔ	ㅔ	ㅔ	
ㅒ	ㅒ	ㅒ	
ㅖ	ㅖ	ㅖ	
ㅢ	ㅢ	ㅢ	

ㅊ	ㅊ	ㅊ		
ㅋ	ㅋ	ㅋ		
ㅌ	ㅌ	ㅌ		
ㅍ	ㅍ	ㅍ		
ㅎ	ㅎ	ㅎ		

Combine the consonants and vowels

	ㅐ	ㅔ	ㅒ	ㅖ	ㅢ
ㅊ	채				
ㅋ		케			
ㅌ			태		
ㅍ				폐	
ㅎ					희

4 Vocabulary

Listen and choose the correct syllable

① ☐ 체   ☐ 케   ☐ 애

② ☐ 희   ☐ 헤   ☐ 의

③ ☐ 채   ☐ 태   ☐ 폐

Listen and repeat the following words

① 개 Dog   ② 가게 Shop   ③ 예의 Etiquette

④ 얘기 Talk   ⑤ 의자 Chair   ⑥ 의사 Doctor

Listen and choose the correct answer

① ☐ 재미 Fun   ☐ 개미 Ant

② ☐ 채소 Vegetable   ☐ 체스 Chess

③ ☐ 스케이트 Skate   ☐ 해바라기 Sunflower

Listen and write the following words

① 대구 Daegu

대	구			

② 세계 World

세	계			

③ 태도 Attitude

태	도			

④ 제주도 Jeju-do

제	주	도		

⑤ 케이크 Cake

케	이	크		

You can now read and say country names in Korean. Listen to the country names shown below and then try reading them aloud.

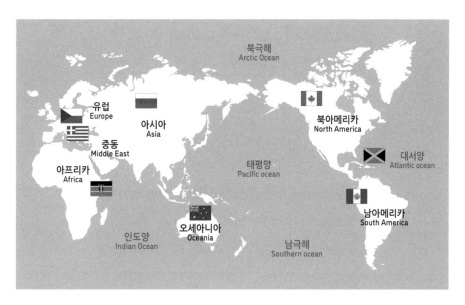

Typing Hangeul on a Mobile Phone

(1) *Dubeolsik* (two-pair layout) on iOS (iPhones)

- Since this mobile keyboard layout is identical to the one used on a computer keyboard, it doesn't take very long to learn or adapt to.
- For the same reason, it's more intuitive and familiar.
- Typing method: similar to that used for a computer keyboard.

(2) *Cheonjiin* keyboard for Android phones

- Syllables are formed by combining the consonants (several of which appear on each key) with the vowel elements ' | ', ' • ', '—' that appear in the first row.
- Those three vowel elements can be used to create all vowel combinations that exist in contemporary Hangeul.
- This keyboard applies the principle of combining *Cheon* (sky, •), *Ji* (earth, —),

and *In* (human, ㅣ) to form Hangeul vowels.

- This may be more accessible to and easier to learn for those who have not yet memorized the entire Hangeul computer keyboard.
- Typing method: input characters in the order of the Korean syllable (initial consonant, middle vowel, final consonant).
  For example: 안녕 → ㅇ + ㅣ + ᆞ + ㄴ / ㄴ + ᆞ + ᆞ + ㅣ + ㅇ

- Press button one time: letter on the left
- Press button two times: letter on the right
- Press button three times: tense consonants (except for ㄴ, ㄹ and ㅇ, ㅁ)

자음	ㄱ	ㄱ	ㄳ	ㄱ + ㅅ
	ㅋ	ㄱ + ㄱ	ㄶ	ㄴ + ㅅ + ㅅ
	ㄲ	ㄱ + ㄱ + ㄱ	ㄺ	ㄴ + ㄴ + ㄱ
			ㄻ	ㄴ + ㄴ + ㅇ + ㅇ

모음	ㅏ	ㅣ + ᆞ	ㅜ	ㅡ + ᆞ
	ㅑ	ㅣ + ᆞ + ᆞ	ㅠ	ㅡ + ᆞ + ᆞ
	ㅐ	ㅣ + ᆞ + ㅣ	ㅝ	ㅡ + ᆞ + ᆞ + ㅣ
	ㅒ	ㅣ + ᆞ + ᆞ + ㅣ	ㅞ	ㅡ + ᆞ + ᆞ + ㅣ + ㅣ
	ㅣ	ㅣ	ㅡ	ㅡ

Combination of 'ㅣ', 'ᆞ' and 'ㅡ'

4

Vowels
and
Consonants ④

Today's Study Plan

Vowels   ㅘ, ㅙ, ㅚ

Consonants ㄲ, ㄸ, ㅃ, ㅆ, ㅉ

와   왜   외

때   꽤   쐬

2   Today's Lesson

Vowels   ㅘ, ㅙ, ㅚ

In this chapter, we will see how previously learned vowels ㅏ, ㅐ, ㅣ
combine with the vowel ㅗ to become ㅘ, ㅙ, ㅚ.

$$\text{ㅗ} + \begin{array}{c} \text{ㅏ} \\ \text{ㅐ} \\ \text{ㅣ} \end{array} = \begin{array}{c} \text{ㅗㅏ} \\ \text{ㅗㅐ} \\ \text{ㅗㅣ} \end{array} \rightarrow \begin{array}{c} \text{ㅘ} \\ \text{ㅙ} \\ \text{ㅚ} \end{array}$$

Here's how these vowels are pronounced and written.

Vowels	IPA	Stroke order
ㅘ	[wa]	
ㅙ	[wɛ]	
ㅚ	[ø/we]	

Earlier, we learned the consonants ㄱ, ㄷ, ㅂ, ㅅ, ㅈ. These consonants can be written twice to produce ㄲ, ㄸ, ㅃ, ㅆ, ㅉ, which are known as double consonants. This can be shown in the table below.

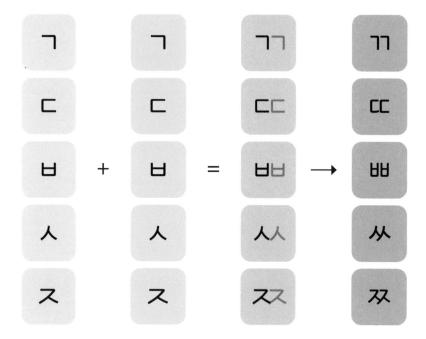

In the previous unit, we learned about the aspirated consonants ㅋ, ㅌ, ㅍ, ㅊ, which are pronounced along with a strong breath of air.
In contrast, the tense consonants ㄲ, ㄸ, ㅃ, ㅆ, ㅉ are pronounced by tensing the vocal cords, as the name applies.

Plain	ㄱ	ㄷ	ㅂ	ㅅ	ㅈ
	[k/g]	[t/d]	[p/b]	[s]	[ts/dz]
Aspirated	ㅋ	ㅌ	ㅍ		ㅊ
	[kʰ]	[tʰ]	[pʰ]		[tsʰ]
Tense	ㄲ	ㄸ	ㅃ	ㅆ	ㅉ
	[k']	[t']	[p']	[s']	[ts']

Let's see how these consonants are pronounced and written.

Consonants	Name	IPA	Stroke order
ㄲ	쌍기역 [ssang-giyeok]	[k']	
ㄸ	쌍디귿 [ssang-digeut]	[t']	
ㅃ	쌍비읍 [ssang-bieup]	[p']	
ㅆ	쌍시옷 [ssang-siot]	[s']	
ㅉ	쌍지읒 [ssang-jieut]	[ts']	

(1) Here are the syllables formed when we combine the vowels (ㅘ, ㅙ, ㅚ) with the silent ㅇ.

(2) Let's take a look at the syllables formed when we combine the vowels (ㅘ, ㅙ, ㅚ) and consonants (ㄲ, ㄸ, ㅃ, ㅆ, ㅉ) we learned in this chapter.

Tutor's tip! The gray letters in the above table are not used much in contemporary Korean.

3 Writing Practice

Vowels					ㅘ, ㅙ, ㅚ

와	❶❷❸❹ 와	와			
왜	❶❷❸❹❺ 왜	왜			
외	❶❷❸ 외	외			

ㄲ	ㄲ	ㄲ			
ㄸ	ㄸ	ㄸ			
ㅃ	ㅃ	ㅃ			
ㅆ	ㅆ	ㅆ			
ㅉ	ㅉ	ㅉ			

Combine the consonants and vowels

	ㅘ	ㅙ	ㅚ
ㄲ	꽈		
ㄸ		뙈	
ㅃ			뾔
ㅆ			
ㅉ			쬐

4 Vocabulary

Listen and choose the correct syllable

① ☐ 꽈   ☐ 쏴   ☐ 쐬

② ☐ 쇠   ☐ 괴   ☐ 왜

③ ☐ 쬐   ☐ 채   ☐ 외

Listen and repeat the following words

① 돼지 Pig   ② 사과 Apple   ③ 꼬리 Tail

④ 코끼리 Elephant   ⑤ 뼈 Bone   ⑥ 최고 Best

Listen and choose the correct answer

① ☐ 아빠 Father   ☐ 아파 It hurts

② ☐ 짜다 Salty   ☐ 자다 To sleep

③ ☐ 싸다 Cheap   ☐ 사다 To buy

Listen and write the following words

① 과자 Snack

과	자			

② 화가 Painter

화	가			

③ 토끼 Rabbit

토	끼			

④ 회사 Company

회	사			

⑤ 쇠고기 Beef

쇠	고	기		

Let's play a game

Let's play *kkeunmaritgi* (word chain) using the words we've learned.

<보기> Example

해바라기
Sunflower
→
기자
Reporter
→
자메이카
Jamaica

교회
Church
→
___사
Company
→
___과
Apple
→
과___
Snack

고기
Meat
→
___자
Reporter
→
___다
To sleep
→
___리미
Iron

<힌트> Hints

기자, 과자, 다리미, 회사, 사과, 자다

5

Vowels
a   n   d
Consonants ⑤

Today's Study Plan

Vowels   ㅋ, ㅖ, ㅟ

Consonants   ㄱ-ㅎ, ㄲ, ㄸ, ㅃ, ㅆ, ㅉ

워	웨	위
줘	훼	귀

2   Today's Lesson

Vowels
ㅝ, ㅞ, ㅟ

The vowels ㅓ, ㅔ, ㅣ, which we've studied previously, combine with the vowel ㅜ to become ㅝ, ㅞ, ㅟ.

ㅜ	+	ㅓ ㅔ ㅣ	=	ㅜㅓ ㅜㅔ ㅜㅣ	→	ㅝ ㅞ ㅟ

Here's how these vowels are pronounced and written.

Vowels	IPA	Stroke order
ㅝ	[wə]	
ㅞ	[we]	
ㅟ	[y/wi]	

Consonants

We've now learned all the consonants in Hangeul.

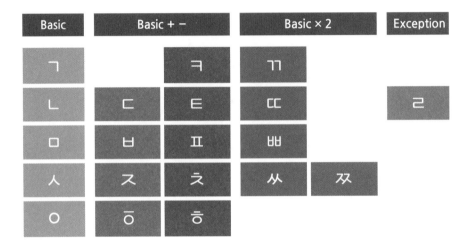

The Hangeul consonants are conventionally arranged as follows.

Vowel + Consonant

(1) Here are the syllables formed when we combine the vowels (ㅝ, ㅞ, ㅟ) with the silent ㅇ.

(2) Here's what we get when we combine the vowels from this unit (ㅝ, ㅞ, ㅟ) with several consonants.

3 Writing Practice

Vowels					ㅓ, ㅔ, ㅜ

ㅝ	ㅝ	ㅝ			
ㅞ	ㅞ	ㅞ			
ㅟ	ㅟ	ㅟ			

88

Consonants

ㄱ	ㄱ				ㅋ	ㅋ		
ㄴ	ㄴ				ㅌ	ㅌ		
ㄷ	ㄷ				ㅍ	ㅍ		
ㄹ	ㄹ				ㅎ	ㅎ		
ㅁ	ㅁ				ㄲ	ㄲ		
ㅂ	ㅂ				ㄸ	ㄸ		
ㅅ	ㅅ				ㅃ	ㅃ		
ㅇ	ㅇ				ㅆ	ㅆ		
ㅈ	ㅈ				ㅉ	ㅉ		
ㅊ	ㅊ							

Combine the consonants and vowels

	ㅝ	ㅞ	ㅟ
ㄱ	궈		
ㄷ			
ㅈ		줴	
ㅎ			
ㄲ			뀌

4 Vocabulary

Listen and choose the correct syllable

① □ 귀   □ 워   □ 눠

② □ 휘   □ 훼   □ 뷔

③ □ 줘   □ 위   □ 뒤

Listen and repeat the following words

① 위 Above   ② 타워 Tower   ③ 더위 Heat

④ 취미 Hobby   ⑤ 가위바위보   ⑥ 꽈배기

　　　　　　　　　　Rock-paper-scissors   Twisted bread stick

Listen and choose the correct answer

① □ 가위 Scissors   □ 거위 Goose

② □ 샤워 Shower   □ 파워 Power

③ □ 지휘자 Conductor   □ 바뀌다 Be changed

Listen and write the following words

① 뛰다 To run

② 쉬다 To rest

③ 스위스 Swiss

④ 웨이터 Waiter

⑤ 스웨터 Sweater

Use the clues below to solve the crossword puzzle.

				③		④ 웨
❶ 기	②		❸	위		
	메		❹	웨		
	❷	마				
	카			⑦ 드		
		⑥		❼	디	오
		❻ 고		마		
❺ 해	⑤					⑧
	지			❽ 다		미

가로 Across
❶ Reporter
❷ Forehead
❸ Scissors
❹ Sweater
❺ Sunflower
❻ Sweet potato
❼ Radio
❽ Iron

세로 Down
① Meat
② Jamaica
③ Swiss
④ Waiter
⑤ Trousers
⑥ Beef
⑦ Drama
⑧ Ant

Answer key

93

Typing Hangeul on a Keyboard

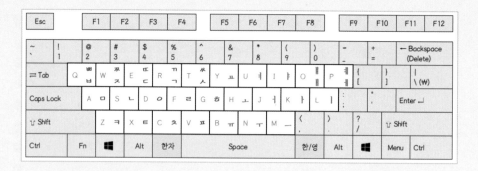

(1) Characteristics of the Korean keyboard

- In the keyboard displayed above, the consonants are grouped on the left and the vowels on the right. This is Korea's standard keyboard layout and the one that's most widely used at present.
- The layout of a Korean keyboard is exactly the same as that of an English keyboard, with the addition of Hangeul displayed alongside the roman alphabet.
- Being the national standard, keyboards of this sort are easy to find in Korea. Most Korean keyboards display letters in *dubeolsik* (two-pair layout). As long as you've memorized the position of the Korean letters, you can easily use an American keyboard to type in Hangeul.

(2) Typing method

- Input characters in the order of the Korean syllable (initial consonant, middle vowel, final consonant).
  (Example: ㅎ + ㅏ + ㄴ + ㄱ + ㅡ + ㄹ → 한글)
- The shift key is used to produce the tense consonants ㄲ, ㄸ, ㅃ, ㅆ, ㅉ. (Example: shift + ㄱ → ㄲ)
- The shift key is also used to produce the double vowels ㅐ, ㅔ.
  (Example: shift + ㅐ → ㅐ)
- To produce the double vowels ㅘ, ㅚ, ㅙ, ㅝ, ㅟ, ㅞ, ㅢ, type the basic vowels in the order they appear. (Example: ㅗ + ㅏ → ㅘ)
- To produce the double batchim ㄳ, ㄵ, ㄶ, ㄼ, ㄳ, ㄾ, ㅀ, ㅄ, ㄺ, ㄻ, ㄿ, type the basic consonants in order. (Example: ㄱ + ㅅ → ㄳ)

- ◆ The "한/영" button is used to switch between Hangeul and Roman letters.
- ◆ The "한자" button is used to convert a Hangeul syllable to a Chinese character.

6

Syllables

Korean Syllable Structure

1 Today's Lesson

◆ Korean Syllables

As we discussed earlier, Hangeul is written in syllable clusters.
Let's look at an example. The word "Hangeul," when written in Hangeul,
is written in two syllable clusters: 한 + 글. In Korean, each syllable
is divided into three parts: initial position, middle position, and final
position.

Initial position: Only consonants are placed here.

Middle position: Only vowels are placed here. Every Korean syllable
must have at least one vowel.

Final position: Only consonants are placed here. This part of the syllable
is called *"batchim"* (받침) in Korean.

◆ The Structure of Korean Syllables

Korean syllables come in four types.

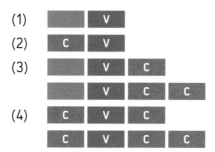

As you can see above, a vowel is the only element that is absolutely required in a Korean syllable. We will examine each of these syllable types in turn.

◆ Syllable Type 1: Vowel

The first Korean syllable type is a syllable that only consists of a vowel. When there's no initial consonant in a Korean syllable, consonant ㅇ is written in the initial position. Note that ㅇ is silent in the initial position.

Tutor's Vowels can make a sound by themselves, even when there's no consonant in
t i p ! the syllable.

◆ Syllable Type 2: Consonant + Vowel

The second Korean syllable type is a syllable in which a consonant is followed by a vowel. Only one consonant can be placed in the initial position.

◆ Syllable Type 3: Vowel + Consonant, Vowel + Consonant + Consonant

The next syllable type is a syllable in which a vowel is followed by one or two consonants.

When there is no initial consonant in a Korean syllable, ㅇ is written in the initial position. Note that ㅇ is silent in the initial position.

Tutor's tip! Vowels can make a sound by themselves, even when there's no consonant in the syllable.

◆ Syllable Type 4: Consonant + Vowel + Consonant, Consonant + Vowel + Consonant + Consonant

The final syllable type is a syllable in which a vowel appears between consonants in the initial and final positions. Only consonants can appear in the initial and final consonants.

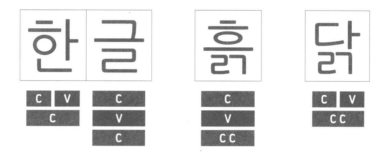

7

Final
Consonants ①

2   Today's Lesson

We have learned about [C | V] earlier in this book.

In this unit, we will add another consonant to that syllable type. The [C] that comes at the end of the syllable in this manner is called *batchim* in Korean.

The written order is as follows: [C] → [V] → [C]

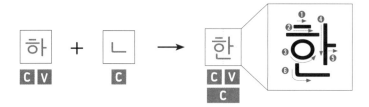

When the consonants ㄱ, ㅋ, ㄲ appear in the final position of a syllable, they're all pronounced as ㄱ (k̚). For example, 악, 앜, and 앆 are all pronounced as [악 (ak̚)].

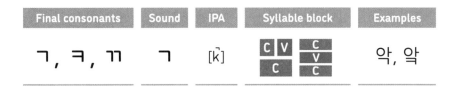

Final consonants	Sound	IPA	Syllable block	Examples
ㄱ, ㅋ, ㄲ	ㄱ	[k̚]	C V / C / C V / C	악, 앜

The following are words with a *batchim* of ㄱ, ㅋ, ㄲ.

Word	Sound value	Writing practice
떡 Ricecake	[떡]	떡
부엌 Kitchen	[부억]	부 엌
밖 Outside	[박]	밖

When the consonants ㄴ, ㄹ, ㅁ appear at the end of a syllable, they are pronounced as follows: ㄴ [n], ㄹ [l], and ㅁ [m].

Final consonants	Sound	IPA	Syllable block	Examples
ㄴ	ㄴ	[n]		안, 온
ㄹ	ㄹ	[l]		알, 올
ㅁ	ㅁ	[m]		암, 옴

The following are words with a *batchim* of ㄴ, ㄹ, ㅁ.

Word	Sound value	Writing practice		
산 Mountain	[산]	산		
달 Moon	[달]	달		
봄 Spring	[봄]	봄		

Final consonants

When the consonants ㅂ, ㅍ appear in the final position of a syllable, they're all pronounced as ㅂ (p̄).

For example, 압 and 앞 are both pronounced as [압 (ap̄)].

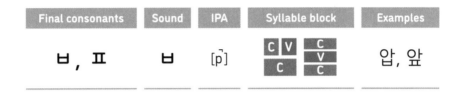

Final consonants	Sound	IPA	Syllable block	Examples
ㅂ, ㅍ	ㅂ	[p̄]		압, 앞

The following are words with a *batchim* of ㅂ, ㅍ.

Word	Sound value	Writing practice			
밥 Rice	[밥]	밥			
앞 Front	[압]	앞			

3   Writing Practice

	ㄱ	악		
아 +	ㅋ	앜		
	ㄲ	앆		

	ㄴ	안		
아 +	ㄹ	알		
	ㅁ	암		

아 +	ㅂ	압			
	ㅍ	앞			

8

Final
Consonants ②

Final consonants

ㄷ, ㅅ, ㅆ, ㅈ, ㅊ, ㅌ, ㅎ / ㅇ

낮	낫	낳
찻	찼	찾
공	창	영

 2 Today's Lesson

Final consonants   ㄷ, ㅅ, ㅆ, ㅈ, ㅊ, ㅌ, ㅎ

Next, we'll be learning about the *batchim* ㄷ, ㅅ, ㅆ, ㅈ, ㅊ, ㅌ, ㅎ. When these consonants appear in the final position of a syllable, they're all pronounced as [ㄷ (t̚)].

For example, 닫, 낫, 났, 낮, 낯, 낱, and 낳 all sound like [낟(nat̚)].

Final consonants	Sound	IPA	Syllable block	Examples
ㄷ, ㅅ, ㅆ, ㅈ, ㅊ, ㅌ, ㅎ	ㄷ	[t̚]		닫, 낫, 났, 낮, 낯, 낱, 낳

The following are words with a *batchim* of ㄷ, ㅅ, ㅆ, ㅈ, ㅊ, ㅌ, ㅎ.

Word	Sound value	Writing practice		
옷 Clothes	[옫]	옷		
꽃 Flower	[꼳]	꽃		
밑 Under	[믿]	밑		
히읗 Korean Letter 'ㅎ'	[히읃]	히	읗	

Let's take a look at the *batchim* ㅇ. When this appears in the final position of a syllable, it's pronounced [ng].

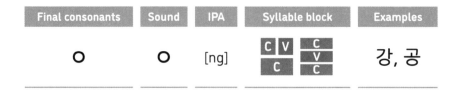

Final consonants	Sound	IPA	Syllable block		Examples
ㅇ	ㅇ	[ng]	C V / C	C / V / C	강, 공

The following are words with *batchim* ㅇ.

Word	Sound value	Writing practice		
공 Ball	[공]	공		
영화 Movie	[영화]	영	화	
창문 Window	[창문]	창	문	
사탕 Candy	[사탕]	사	탕	

Final consonants ㄷ, ㅅ, ㅆ, ㅈ, ㅊ, ㅌ, ㅎ

아 +		
ㄷ	앋	
ㅅ	앗	
ㅆ	았	
ㅈ	앚	
ㅊ	앛	
ㅌ	앝	
ㅎ	앟	

Final consonants ㅇ

아 +	ㅇ	앙

9

Final
Consonants ③

1 Listening

앉   없   않

값   닭   밝

2 Today's Lesson

Final consonants   ㄳ, ㄵ, ㄶ, ㄼ, ㄽ, ㄾ, ㅀ, ㅄ / ㄺ, ㄻ, ㄿ

When two consonants appear under the vowel in the final position of a syllable, they're called a double *batchim*.

C	V
CC	

ㅁ	ㅏ
ㄴ	ㅎ

C	ㅎ
V	ㅜ
C C	ㄹㅌ

Double *batchim* are written in the following order.

 + →

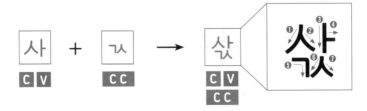

118

While double *batchim* consist of two consonants, usually only one of them is pronounced. The first consonant is pronounced in ㄳ, ㄵ, ㄶ, ㄼ, ㄽ, ㄾ, ㅀ, ㅄ, and the second consonant is pronounced in ㄺ, ㄻ, ㄿ.

Pronunciation	Final consonant	Sound	IPA	Examples
First consonant is pronounced	ㄳ	ㄱ	[k̚]	삯
	ㄵ	ㄴ	[n]	앉
	ㄶ			많
	ㄼ	ㄹ	[l]	넓
	ㄽ			곬
	ㄾ			핥
	ㅀ			싫
	ㅄ	ㅂ	[p̚]	값
Second consonant is pronounced	ㄺ	ㄱ	[k̚]	닭
	ㄻ	ㅁ	[m]	삶
	ㄿ	ㅍ	[p̚]	읊

Final consonants   ㄱㅅ, ㄴㅈ, ㄴㅎ, ㄹㅂ, ㄹㅅ, ㄹㅌ, ㄹㅎ, ㅂㅅ / ㄹㄱ, ㄹㅁ, ㄹㅍ

삯	삯
앉	앉
않	않
밟	밟
곬	곬
핥	핥
싫	싫
없	없
닭	닭
삶	삶
읊	읊

Listen and choose the correct syllable

① ☐ 악   ☐ 각   ☐ 박

② ☐ 갑   ☐ 감   ☐ 각

③ ☐ 밖   ☐ 앉   ☐ 삵

Listen and repeat the following words

① 입 [입] Mouth   ② 부엌 [부억] Kitchen

③ 가방 [가방] Bag   ④ 히읗 [히읃] Korean alphabet 'ㅎ'

⑤ 값 [갑] Price   ⑥ 시간 [시간] Time

⑦ 을지로 [을지로] Euljiro   ⑧ 여덟 [여덜] Eight

Listen and write the following words

① 가족 Family

가	족				

② 엄마 Mom

엄	마				

③ 한국 Korea

한	국				

④ 걷다 To walk

걷	다				

⑤ 영화 Movie

영	화				

⑥ 꽃 Flower

꽃					

⑦ 읽다 To read

읽	다				

⑧ 앉다 To sit

앉	다				

⑨ 맑다 Clear

맑	다				

Let's play a game

1. The neighborhood of Insa-dong, located in the heart of Seoul, is a fascinating place where visitors can encounter traditional products, restaurants, and galleries.

While store signs in Korea are often written in the roman alphabet, most of the signs in Insa-dong are written in Hangeul. Insa-dong store signs appear in the following photographs. Try matching the store signs written in Hangeul with the corresponding English names.

●   ● Starbucks

●   ● GS 25

●   ● KT

●   ● CU

Answer key

● CU   ●

● KT   ●

● GS 25   ●

● Starbucks   ●

124

2. Below is a map of Korea. As you listen to the recording, play a game of bingo using Korean city names.

대구	울산	속초	춘천
원주	서울	안동	인천
강릉	대전	부산	전주
보령	경주	제주도	창원

How Koreans Greet Each Other

How do people greet each other in Korea? When meeting someone for the first time or running into a friend on the street, Koreans typically bow at the waist at 15–30 degrees. In Korea, a bow of this sort signifies humility and respect.

While Koreans often bow from the waist when greeting others, this isn't necessarily done every time. When Koreans run into a close colleague, meet several people at the same time, or greet someone in a tight space, they're more likely to simply make eye contact and nod their head. Koreans call this *nun-insa* (눈인사), or literally "eye greeting." Just like bowing from the waist, nodding your head is also considered a courteous form of greeting.

Jeol, Korea's traditional greeting

Traditionally, Jeol (절), meaning a deep bow, has been the most courteous and respectful way of greeting another person in Korea. This indoor bow is performed by kneeling down and then lowering one's head to the floor. In contemporary society, such deep bows are reserved for special occasions, including weddings, ancestral ceremonies, and major holidays such as Seollal (the Lunar New Year) and Chuseok (the Autumn Harvest Festival).

Tutor's tip !

How to greet a Korean

1) Look the other person in the eye.

2) Bend slightly at the waist.

3) As you straighten, say, "Annyeonghaseyo?" (안녕하세요?)

→ This expression and other Korean greetings will be covered in the next unit.

Introducing

Yourself

Throughout each stage, you will study the basic grammatical constructions and vocabulary needed to introduce yourself, until you're ready to make a simple self-introduction.

1
Greetings

Today's Study Plan

안녕하세요?

만나서 반갑습니다.

How to Introduce Yourself in Korean

In this unit, you'll learn how to say hello and introduce
yourself when meeting someone for the first time.
The focus here will be on formal greetings.

1   Greetings

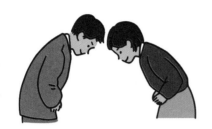

A: 안녕하세요?

B: 안녕하세요?

A: 만나서 반갑습니다.

B: 반갑습니다.

 2   Today's Lesson

Let's learn how to say hello in Korean.

"안녕하세요?" is the expression used to say hello to someone.

"만나서 반갑습니다" or "만나서 반가워요" is the greeting used when meeting someone for the first time.

"안녕히 가세요" and "안녕히 계세요" are greetings used when saying goodbye to someone.

Tutor's tip!   "안녕하세요?" can be used at any time without distinguishing between the morning, afternoon, or evening.

"안녕히 가세요" is spoken to the person(s) leaving.

"안녕히 계세요" is spoken to the person(s) staying.

When both parties are leaving at the same time, they should both say "안녕히 가세요"

"고맙습니다" and "감사합니다" are used to express gratitude, as in the expression "Thank you."

"미안합니다" and "죄송합니다" are used to acknowledge a mistake or express a feeling of remorse, as in the expression "I'm sorry."

Honorific expression	Situation	Casual speech
안녕하세요?	When meeting someone	안녕?
안녕히 가세요.	When saying farewell	안녕. 잘 가.
안녕히 주무세요.	When saying goodnight / before going to bed	잘 자.
고맙습니다. 감사합니다.	When expressing gratitude	고마워.
미안합니다. 죄송합니다.	When apologizing	미안해.

Tutor's tip! A distinctive characteristic of the Korean language is its honorifics. Grammar and vocabulary can change depending on the relative situation, status, and age of the people in a conversation. Speakers use honorifics to express respect for the other person or their social relationship with their audience or listener in respect to such factors as age, social status, gender, intimacy, and the nature of the conversation itself.

2

Name

Today's Study Plan

이름이 뭐예요?

저는 스테판이에요.

This is how to tell someone your name in Korean.

이름이 뭐예요?
What is your name?

저는 스테판이에요.
I am Stephen.

Grammar 1 이름이 뭐예요?

이름이 뭐예요?
What is your name?

저는 스테판이에요.
I am Stephen.

이름이 뭐예요?
What is your name?

제 이름은 김누리예요.
My name is Nuri Kim.

만나서 반가워요.
Nice to meet you.

만나서 반가워요.
Nice to meet you.

The nouns is followed by "-이에요" when they end in a *batchim* and by
"-예요" when they do not.

가원
　　　　　+　　이에요.
스테판

누리
　　　　　+　　예요.
아이유

Tutor's tip!

Here are two ways to tell someone your name in Korean.

① 저는 + 스테판 + 이에요.　　→　저는 스테판이에요.
② 제 이름은 + 스테판 + 이에요.　→　제 이름은 스테판이에요.

2   Introducing Yourself

When you become acquainted with a Korean, you can now say hello and introduce yourself.

Example

이름: 김누리

안녕하세요?

저는 김누리예요.

만나서 반가워요.

이름: 오스만

저는

만나서 반가워요.

이름: 매튜

제 이름은

이름: 아이샤

Forms of Address Used in Korea

Koreans don't call each other by their plain given name unless they're close friends. Instead, various forms of address are used, such as placing the honorific suffixes "-님" and "-씨" after a job title or name. It's also possible to address a close friend who is older than you with family terms normally used for older brothers ("형" and "오빠") and older sisters ("언니" and "누나").

- name/title + 님 (Mr./Ms. in English): used to express respect to an older individual

- name + -씨: used to express courtesy and maintain formality

- family terms for older brothers and sisters: used to address older people who are not family members

---

- 형/오빠 (older brother): While these are normally used among family members, they can also be used when addressing an older man, as long as the age gap is not too large.
- 누나/언니 (older sister): While these are normally used among family members, they can also be used when addressing an older woman, as long as the age gap is not too large.
- 형/누나: terms of address used by a male speaker
- 오빠/언니: terms of address used by a female speaker

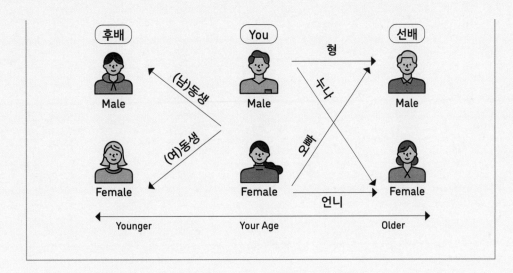

- Family terms can be used by themselves, or they can be used after the name. (Example: 형 or 스테판 형)

- When the speaker is addressing someone who is younger or a close friend, they often call them by their name (provided that they're in a close relationship). (Example: 한국아, 누리야)

3
Nationality

어느 나라 사람이에요?

저는 프랑스 사람이에요.

The phrase used to ask someone where they're from is "어느 나라," which literally means "which country." To answer this question, you can say the name of your country followed by the word "사람" (person).

어느 나라 사람이에요?
Where are you from?

저는 프랑스 사람이에요.
I am from France.

Grammar 어느 나라 사람이에요?

저는	나라 country	사람 person	이에요.
	한국 Korea		
	미국 USA		
	프랑스 France		
	인도 India		

2 Vocabulary: Countries

캐나다	영국	튀르키예	한국
Canada	United Kingdom	Türkiye	Republic of Korea

미국	프랑스	베트남	중국
USA	France	Vietnam	China

브라질	이집트	호주	일본
Brazil	Egypt	Australia	Japan

3   Introducing Yourself

Now, when becoming acquainted with a Korean, you can tell them what country you're from.

Example

이름: 김누리
국적: 한국

안녕하세요?

저는 김누리예요.

저는 한국 사람이에요.

이름: 오스만
국적: 튀르키예

저는

저는　　　　　사람이에요.

이름: 매튜
국적: 호주

안녕하세요?

제 이름은

저는

이름: 아이샤
국적: 인도네이사

4

Occupation

직업이 뭐예요?

저는 학생이에요.

This is how Koreans tell each other what job they have.

직업이 뭐예요?
What is your occupation?

저는 학생이에요.
I am a student.

Grammar   직업이 뭐예요?

	직업 occupation	이에요. / 예요.
저는	선생님 a teacher	이에요.
	학생 a student	
	의사 a doctor	예요.
	가수 a singer	

Tutor's tip! The nouns above are followed by "-이에요" when they end in a *batchim* and by "-예요" when they do not.

선생님	학생	회사원	예술가
Teacher	Student	Office worker	Artist

개발자	의사	간호사	경찰
Software engineer	Doctor	Nurse	Police

가수	디자이너	요리사	건축가
Singer	Designer	Cook/ Chef	Architect

운동선수	프로게이머	변호사	배우
Athlete	Professional gamer	Lawyer	Actor

작가	과학자	농부	기자
Writer	Scientist	Farmer	Reporter

When you make the acquaintance of a Korean, you can now tell them what your job is.

Example

이름: 김누리
국적: 한국
직업: 선생님

안녕하세요?

저는 김누리예요.

저는 선생님이에요.

이름: 오스만
국적: 튀르키예
직업: 가수

저는

저는　　　　　　　예요.

이름: 매튜
국적: 호주
직업: 프로게이머

안녕하세요?

제 이름은

저는

이름: 아이샤
국적: 인도네시아
직업: 회사원

Metal Chopsticks Are Unique to Korea

Korean dining culture is based on spoons and chopsticks. Spoons are used to eat rice and soup, while chopsticks are used to eat the side dishes. Spoon (숟가락) and chopsticks (젓가락) together can be abbreviated as "수저," roughly meaning "silverware."

Korean Silverware

Korea's neighboring countries, including China, Japan, and Vietnam, also use chopsticks, but each country's chopsticks are shaped differently. In China, chopsticks are long and thick; in Japan, they have pointed ends. Additionally, both countries use wooden chopsticks, while Korean chopsticks are made of metal. Curiously enough, Korea is the only country in the world that uses metal chopsticks.

In China, family members sit around the table and serve themselves from communal dishes placed in the middle of the table, far from their individual plates. For that reason, and because of the numerous deep-fried and stir-fried dishes in Chinese cuisine, Chinese chopsticks became long and thick.

In Japan it isn't customary to share food from communal dishes. Instead, Japanese people eat from rice bowls, soup bowls, and side dish plates placed directly in front of them. As a result, Japanese chopsticks are on the shorter side. Japanese chopsticks also tend to be pointy to make eating common dishes easier such as bony fish, shellfish, and noodle dishes like udon.

Koreans have long been proficient at making and using metal tools. People in Korea tend to eat a lot of vegetable dishes, including kimchi, and so they came to use metal chopsticks with flat ends, to help maintain a good grip on the food they pick up. Metal chopsticks are also extremely durable and can be used for a long time.

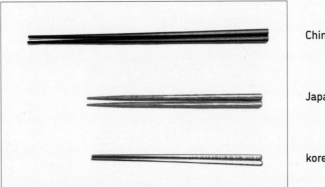

Chinese chopsticks

Japanese chopsticks

korean chopsticks

Tutor's tip ! Pushing around side dishes with your chopsticks is considered bad manners in Korea. Korean table manners also require you to wait for the oldest person at the table to begin eating before you can dig in.

5

Hobbies

취미가 뭐예요?

제 취미는 운동이에요.

저는 조깅을 좋아해요.

1   Today's Lesson

This is how Koreans tell each other what hobbies they have.

취미가 뭐예요?
What is your hobby?

제 취미는 운동이에요.
My hobby is exercising.
저는 조깅을 좋아해요.
I like jogging.

Grammar 1   취미가 뭐예요?

	취미 hobby (Noun)	이에요. / 예요.
제 취미는	운동 sport	이에요.
	요리 cooking	예요.

Grammar 2   무슨 N (hobby)을/를 좋아해요?

	취미 hobby (Noun)	을/를 좋아해요.
저는	조깅 jogging	을 좋아해요.
	한국 요리 Korean cuisine	를 좋아해요.

Grammar 3   N을/를

"-을/를" is the object particle in Korean. That is to say, the noun that "-을/를" is placed after is the object of the sentence. This particle is written as "을" when the noun ends in a *batchim* and as "를" when it does not.

Noun with batchim + 을	Noun without batchim + 를
운동 등산 + 을 음악	낚시 요가 + 를 노래

운동 Sport	영화보기 Watching movies	음악 듣기 Listening to music	기타 ETC
야구 Baseball	로맨스 영화 Romantic movie	K-pop K-pop	쇼핑 Shopping
태권도 Taekwondo	공포 영화 Horror movie	팝송 Pop	여행 Traveling
요가 Yoga	코미디 영화 Comedy movie	재즈 Jazz	캠핑 Camping
수영 Swimming	액션 영화 Action movie	클래식 Classical music	게임 Playing games

3   Introducing Yourself

When becoming acquainted with a Korean, you can now tell them what your hobby is.

Example

이름: 김누리
국적: 한국
직업: 선생님
취미: 영화 보기/액션 영화

저는 김누리예요.

제 취미는 영화 보기예요.

저는 액션 영화를 좋아해요.

이름: 오스만
국적: 튀르키예
직업: 가수
취미: 음악 듣기/K-pop

저는

제 취미는

저는   좋아해요.

이름: 매튜
국적: 호주
직업: 프로게이머
취미: 여행/ 캠핑

제 이름은

제 취미는 여행이에요.

저는

이름: 아이샤
국적: 인도네이사
직업: 회사원
취미: 운동/ 태권도

6
Introducing
Yourself

Today's Study Plan

You can use the grammar constructions and vocabulary you've learned so far to make a simple self-introduction.

So far, we've learned simple sentences you can use to introduce yourself when meeting someone for the first time. Let's go over them once again.

Dialogue

안녕하세요?
저는 김누리예요.
만나서 반가워요.

안녕하세요?
제 이름은 스테판이에요.
만나서 반가워요.

스테판 씨는
어느 나라 사람이에요?

저는 프랑스 사람이에요.
누리 씨는 어느 나라 사람이에요?

저는 한국 사람이에요.
저는 선생님이에요.
스테판 씨는 직업이 뭐예요?

저는 학생이에요.
누리 씨는 취미가 뭐예요?

제 취미는 영화 보기예요.

무슨 영화를 좋아해요?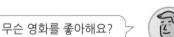

저는 액션 영화를 좋아해요.
스테판 씨는 취미가 뭐예요?

제 취미는 운동이에요.
저는 조깅을 좋아해요.

You can now introduce yourself using the sentences you've learned so far.

Example

이름: 김누리
국적: 한국
직업: 선생님
취미: 영화 보기/액션 영화

안녕하세요?

제 이름은 김누리예요.

저는 한국 사람이에요.

저는 선생님이에요.

제 취미는 영화 보기예요.

저는 액션 영화를 좋아해요.

만나서 반가워요.

이름:
국적:
직업:
취미:

Koreans' Use of *Ondol* (Floor Heating)

● **Heating methods in Korea**

Most houses in Korea make use of the *ondol** method of floor heating. This involves heating the entire floor, which then indirectly heats the air above it. While *ondol* system was used to heat the floor with smoke from a wood furnace, nowadays a boiler is used to heat water that runs through the floor. Floor heating also contributed to the development of Koreans' customs of sitting on the floor and walking barefoot in the house.

Because an *ondol* system heats the entire floor, Koreans prefer heaters that transfer heat directly to the body. In the cold winter months, they like to warm up by lying down on the toasty floor. One interesting way to experience Korean bathing culture is by visiting a *jjimjilbang* (찜질방). These facilities have sauna rooms where water is steamed over red clay or charcoal and the floors are heated with the *ondol* system mentioned above.

* *Ondol* (온돌): a traditional Korean method of heating the floor

Floor culture

Korean *jjimjilbang*

● Modern Korean houses

Because Korean houses heat all their floors using an *ondol* system, a strict distinction is maintained between inside and outside spaces. When people go inside, they take off their shoes. Since the floor is kept warm in the winter, people can just leave the floor bare without bothering with carpets or mats. If you visit the house of a Korean friend, be sure to take off your shoes before going inside!

Strict distinction between inside and outside

Living room of a modern apartment

ANSWER

Vowels and Consonants ❶

Listen and choose the correct syllable

1. 가   2. 마   3. 나

Listen and choose the correct answer

1. 나무   2. 아니   3. 고기

Vowels and Consonants ❷

Listen and choose the correct syllable

1. 댜   2. 료   3. 쥬

Listen and choose the correct answer

1. 이유   2. 여자   3. 다리미

Vowels and Consonants ❸

Listen and choose the correct syllable

1. 체   2. 희   3. 태

Listen and choose the correct answer

1. 재미   2. 채소   3. 해바라기

Vowels and Consonants ❹

Listen and choose the correct syllable

1. 꽈   2. 괴   3. 쬐

Listen and choose the correct answer

1. 아빠   2. 짜다   3. 사다

Vowels and Consonants ❺

Listen and choose the correct syllable

1. 워   2. 뷔   3. 쥐

Listen and choose the correct answer

1. 거위   2. 파워   3. 바뀌다

Final consonants

Listen and choose the correct syllable

1. 악   2. 감   3. 밖

INDEX

2. Vowels and Consonants ❷

교수	Professor
기자	Reporter
다리미	Iron
드라마	Drama
무료	Free of charge
바지	Trousers
서류	Document
아니요	No
야구	Baseball
여우	Fox
여자	Woman
요리	Cooking
우유	Milk
유리	Glass
이유	Reason
주유소	Gas station

3. Vowels and Consonants ❸

가게	Shop
개	Dog
개미	Ant
그리스	Greece

INDEX

4. Vowels and Consonants ❹

과자	Snack
교회	Church
꼬리	Tail
돼지	Pig
뼈	Bone
사과	Apple
사다	To buy
쇠고기	Beef
싸다	Cheap
아빠	Father
아파	It hurts.
자다	To sleep
짜다	Salty
최고	Best
코끼리	Elephant
토끼	Rabbit
화가	Painter
회사	Company

5. Vowels and Consonants ❺

가위	Scissors
가위바위보	Rock-paper-scissors

INDEX

6. Syllables

7. Final Consonants ❶

달	Moon
떡	Ricecake
밖	Outside
밥	Rice
봄	Spring
부엌	Kitchen
산	Mountain
앞	Front

8. Final Consonants ❷

공	Ball
꽃	Flower
밑	Under
사탕	Candy
영화	Movie
옷	Clothes
창문	Window
히읗	Korean letter 'ㅎ'

9. Final Consonants ❸

가방	Bag
가족	Family
값	Price
강릉	Gangneung
걷다	To walk
경주	Gyeongju
남해	South Sea
대전	Daejeon
동해	East Sea
맑다	Clear
보령	Boryeong
부산	Busan
서울	Seoul
서해	West Sea
속초	Sokcho
시간	Time
안동	Andong
앉다	To sit
엄마	Mom
여덟	Eight
울산	Ulsan
원주	Wonju
을지로	Euljiro
인천	Incheon

읽다	To read
입	Mouth
전주	Jeonju
창원	Changwon
춘천	Chuncheon
한국	Republic of Korea

Introducing Yourself

1. Greeting

인사	Greetings
감사합니다.	Thank you.
고마워.	Thank you.
고맙습니다.	Thank you.
만나서 반가워요.	Nice to meet you.
만나서 반갑습니다.	Nice to meet you.
미안합니다.	Sorry.
미안해.	Sorry.
반갑습니다.	Nice to meet you.
안녕.	Hello.
안녕하세요.	Hello.
안녕히 가세요.	Good-bye.

INDEX

안녕히 계세요.	Good-bye.
안녕히 주무세요.	Good night.
잘 가.	Good-bye.
잘 자.	Good night.
죄송합니다.	Sorry.

2. Name

이름	Name
이름이 뭐예요?	What is your name?

3. Nationality

나라	Country
어느 나라 사람이에요?	Where are you from?
국적	Nationality
미국	U.S.A
베트남	Vietnam
브라질	Brazil
사람	Person
영국	United Kingdom
이집트	Egypt
인도	India

인도네시아	Indonesia
일본	Japan
중국	China
캐나다	Canada
튀르키예	Türkiye
프랑스	France
한국	Republic of Korea
호주	Australia

4. Occupation

직업	Occupation
직업이 뭐예요?	What is your occupation?
가수	Singer
간호사	Nurse
개발자	Software Engineer
건축가	Architect
경찰	Police
과학자	Scientist
기자	Reporter
농부	Farmer
디자이너	Designer
배우	Actor
변호사	Lawyer
선생님	Teacher

INDEX

예술가	Artist
요리사	Cook/ Chef
운동선수	Athlete
의사	Doctor
작가	Writer
프로게이머	Professional Gamer
학생	Student
회사원	Office worker

5. Hobbies

취미	Hobby
취미가 뭐예요?	What is your hobby?
K-pop	K-pop
게임	Playing games
공포 영화	Horror movie
기타	ETC
낚시	Fishing
노래	Song/Singing
등산	Hiking
로맨스 영화	Romantic movie
쇼핑	Shopping
수영	Swimming
액션 영화	Action movie

여행	Traveling
영화 보기	Watching movies
요가	Yoga
요리	Cooking
운동	Sport
음악	Music
음악 듣기	Listening to music
재즈	Jazz
조깅	Jogging
캠핑	Camping
코미디 영화	Comedy movie
클래식	Classical music
태권도	Taekwondo
팝송	Pop song
한국 요리	Korean cuisine

MEMO

OH! MY KOREAN TUTORS

Copyright © 2025 by Yoonjun Kim, Hyunju Nam, Gail Yoon, Seonkyong Lee
Consultant: Minwoo Lee (Professor in the Department of Korean
at Cyber Hankuk University of Foreign Studies)

Published in 2025 by Seoul Selection
B1, 6 Samcheong-ro, Jongno-gu, Seoul 03062, Korea
Phone   (82-2) 734-9567
Fax   (82-2) 734-9563
Email   hankinseoul@gmail.com
Website   www.seoulselection.com

ISBN: 979-11-89809-76-8 13710
Printed in the Republic of Korea